SPANISH CULTURAL CHALLENGE

190 Brainteasers *for* Beginning *and* Intermediate Spanish Students

Cathy Wilson and William A. Fleig

GOOD YEAR BOOKS

are available for most basic curriculum subjects plus many enrichment areas. For more Good Year Books, contact your local bookseller or educational dealer. For a complete catalog with information about other Good Year Books, please contact:

Good Year Books
P.O. Box 91858
Tucson, AZ 85752-1858
www.goodyearbooks.com

ISBN: 1-59647-051-8

Illustrations: Nancy Rudd
Design: Daniel Miedaner

Spanish challenge

Cultural

Fact!

There are seven countries in Central America. Spanish is the official language in all except one.

Name the countries in Central America. Which one has English as its official language?

1. Guatemala, 2. Belize, 3. El Salvador, 4. Honduras, 5. Nicaragua, 6. Costa Rica, 7. Panama; Belize

Really?

Christopher Columbus (known in Spanish as Cristóbal Colón) was born in Italy. Yet the King and Queen of Spain gave him the money for his voyage to the New World.

What were the names of the Spanish king and queen who funded his voyage?

Ferdinand and Isabella (*Fernando e Isabel*)

    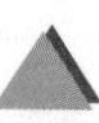  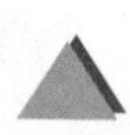

Cool!

This world-famous Spanish singer has sold more records than any other male singer—even Frank Sinatra! A former soccer player, he began to play the guitar while recuperating from a car accident. And the rest, as they say, is history!

What is the name of this popular singer?

Julio Iglesias

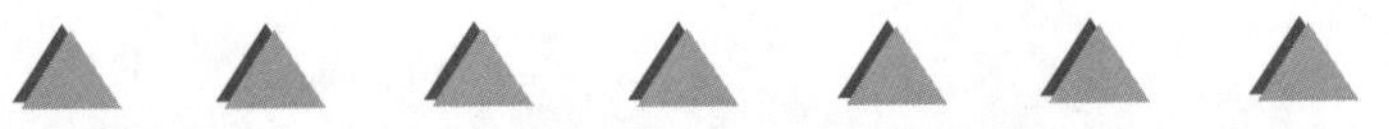

Spanish challenge **Cultural**

Cultural Spanish challenge

Listen!

From February 23 to March 6, 1836, a band of 189 men defended this fort against an attack by 4,000 Mexican soldiers led by General Santa Anna. Among the fort's defenders were such famous frontiersmen as Davy Crockett and Jim Bowie. All of the men lost their lives when the fort fell.

What was the name of this fort? What modern Texas city has grown up around it?

Look!

This Spanish explorer led the first European expedition to reach what is now Florida. In 1513 he explored much of the area while searching for the legendary Fountain of Youth.

What is the name of this Spanish explorer?

7

Ponce de León

Really?

In 1565 the Spanish established a fort in northeastern Florida. Today it is the oldest continuously existing city in the United States.

What is the name of this city?

St. Augustine (*San Agustín*)

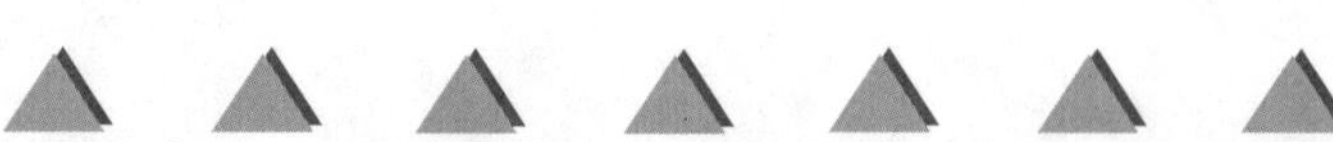

Spanish challenge Cultural

Fact!

Washington, D.C., is the headquarters of this organization that provides for collective self-defense, cooperation, and peace among Latin American countries and the United States.

What is the name of the organization?

Organization of American States (O.A.S.)

Look!

Body language is a nonverbal means of communication. In Hispanic cultures, there are many unique forms of body language.

You see someone from Mexico place the index finger under his eye, pull down slightly, and say *"¡Ojo!"* What do you think this person is saying?

Be careful! Watch out!

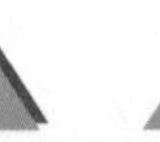

Spanish challenge **Cultural**

Look!

This gesture is common in Mexico. A person might use it to describe someone's attitude toward money.

You see a person tap her elbow with the palm of her hand. What do you think she is saying about someone else's attitude toward money?

That person is cheap!

Really?

In the Spanish-speaking world, Christmas Day is a purely religious holiday. January 6 is the day for gift giving and is called el *Día de los Reyes,* which means Day of the Kings.

Why do you think the holiday is called that? As part of the celebration, children may put straw in their shoes. Why?

It celebrates the day the Three Kings, or Wise Men, arrived in Bethlehem; the straw will provide food for the Kings' camels

   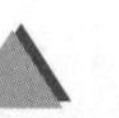 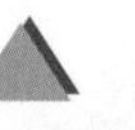 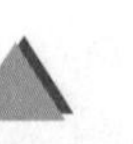 

Fact!

Mexican Independence Day is September 16. In 1810, a priest named Miguel Hidalgo shouted the famous *"¡Viva México!"* that urged people on to revolution.

From which country was Mexico fighting for independence? In what year did Mexico gain its independence?

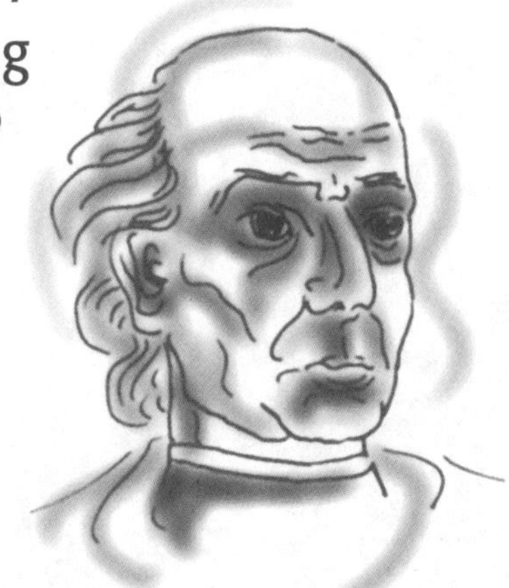

Spain; 1821

Listen!

A very popular event takes place in Spain at 4:00 on Sunday afternoons (as well as at other times). This event is also popular in other Spanish-speaking countries. If you were to attend, you would be going to *la corrida* at *la Plaza de Toros.*

What are you going to see and where are you going to see it?

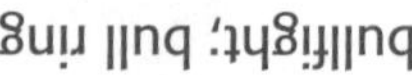

Neat!

Baja California is a long peninsula known for its beautiful beaches, blue waters, and abundant fishing. It is becoming a very popular tourist destination.

Where is Baja California? What country is it part of? Which large body of water is on its west coast?

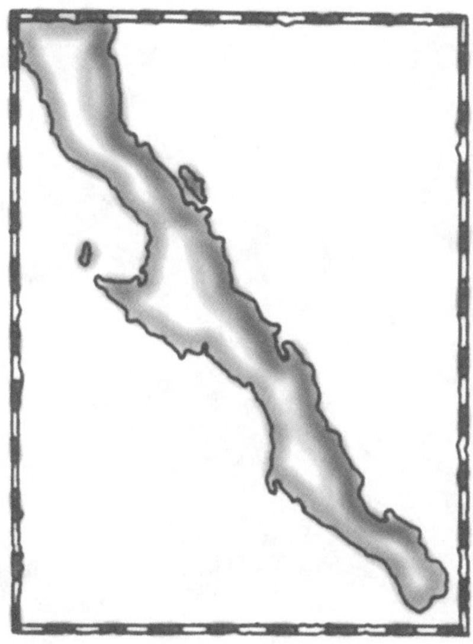

directly south of California; Mexico;
Pacific Ocean

Really?

Did you know that olive oil is one of the most healthful oils available?

What Spanish-speaking country is the world's leading commercial producer of olives? Why do you think some olives are green and others are black?

Spain; black ones are ripe and green ones are not

     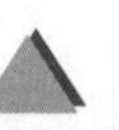 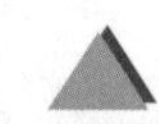

Who Knew?

Aconcagua is the highest mountain in South America. It rises 6,959 meters above sea level.

In what mountain range and in which country is Aconcagua located?

17

Andes Mountains; Argentina

Cultural Spanish challenge

Who Knew?

One of the driest places on earth is the Atacama Desert. It receives less than half an inch of rain yearly.

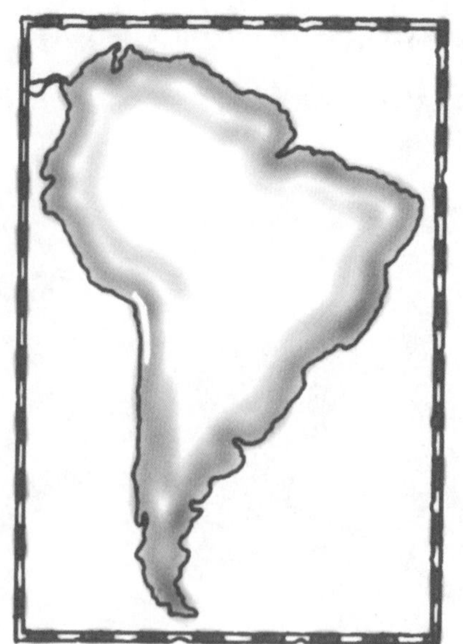

The Atacama Desert is found in which two South American countries?

Chile and Peru

Cool!

The Galapagos Islands are famous for being the home of unusual birds, tortoises, and the Galapagos marine iguana.

What country are the Galapagos Islands part of? What famous scientist developed his theories after visiting these islands?

Ecuador; Charles Darwin

Spanish challenge **Cultural**

Cultural Spanish challenge

Fact!

The country of Ecuador is located in South America between Colombia and Peru. Its capital is Quito.

Why do you think the country is named Ecuador? Is its coastline on the Atlantic or Pacific Ocean?

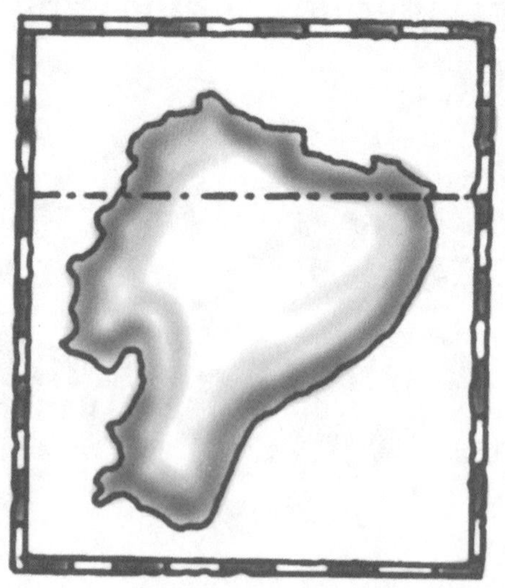

The equator (*el ecuador*) passes through it; Pacific Ocean

 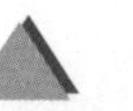  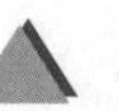 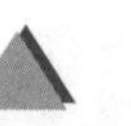 

Listen!

If you enjoy Mexican cuisine, you are surely familiar with this fruit. Among its many varieties are *poblano, serrano, habanero,* and *jalapeño.*

What is this food? Which of the varieties is sometimes called "the most dreaded?"

peppers; *habanero*

Cultural Spanish challenge

Neat!

One of the benefits of travel is eating foods that are not common—or may even be unknown—in the United States. If you traveled in Central America, you would have a chance to try a guayaba, mamey, or mango.

What type of food would you be eating?

fruit

Spanish challenge **Cultural**

Listen!

This humanitarian organization is often the first to bring aid when a disaster occurs. Its symbol is recognized and welcomed around the world.

Known in Spanish as *la Cruz Roja,* what is its name in English?

23

the Red Cross

Cultural Spanish challenge

Fact!

Corn *(el maíz)* has been a very important staple in Latin America since pre-Columbian times.

Can you think of three Mexican dishes that use *maíz* as a main ingredient?

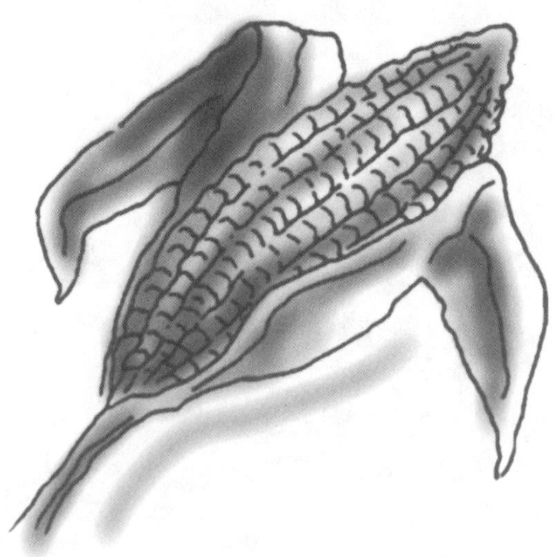

tortillas, tacos, tamales, enchiladas,
sopa de tortilla, chilaquiles

Weird!

A very popular dish in Central America and the Caribbean is black beans and rice. In many places this is known as *moros y cristianos* (Moors and Christians).

To what historical period does this name refer?

25

the period in which the Arabs occupied Spain (711–1492)

Cool!

The cuisine of Spain can be found in countries around the world. How well do you know Spanish food? Can you match the dish to its description?

flan	a. cold vegetable soup that includes oil, vinegar, and garlic
gazpacho	b. baked custard with caramel sauce
paella	c. chicken, seafood, and rice dish seasoned with saffron (a yellow spice)
tortilla española	d. potato omelet

flan–b; *gazpacho*–a; *paella*–c; *tortilla española*–d

Look!

An isthmus is a strip of land that connects two larger bodies of land and that has water on both sides. Panama is an isthmus, now separated into two parts by the Panama Canal.

Which two continents does Panama connect? What two bodies of water does the canal connect?

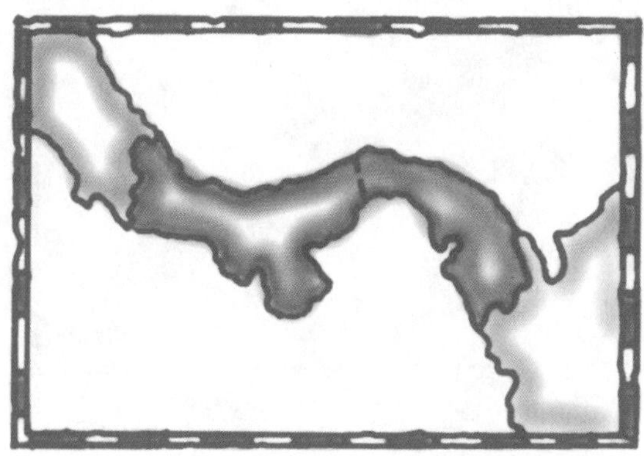

North and South America; Pacific Ocean and Caribbean Sea

Spanish challenge

Cultural

Fact!

Mexico and the United States share a common border. Part of the border is a river.

What is the name of the river that separates Mexico and the United States? What large body of water does the river flow into?

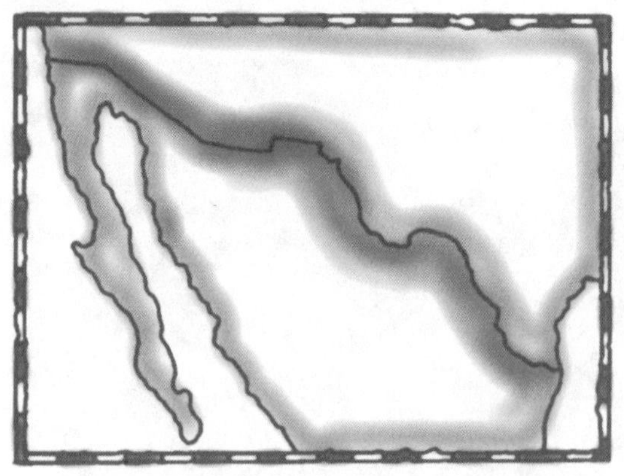

Rio Grande (Río Bravo); Gulf of Mexico

Listen!

There are two countries on the Caribbean island of Hispaniola. One is a Spanish-speaking country; the other is not.

What is the Spanish-speaking country that shares the island of Hispaniola: What is the other country? What two languages are spoken there?

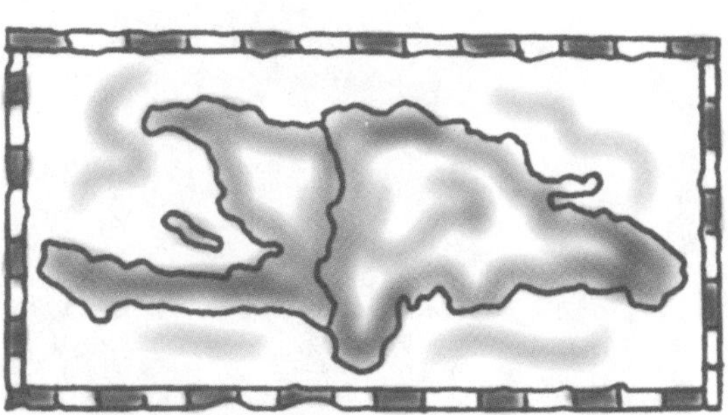

the Dominican Republic; Haiti; French and Creole

Spanish challenge Cultural

Cultural Spanish challenge

Fact!

Cities in the United States and some Spanish-speaking countries share similar latitudes or longitudes.

Which city is farther north—New York City or Madrid, Spain? Which is farther east—Miami, Florida, or Havana, Cuba? Which is farther west—Los Angeles, California, or Santiago, Chile?

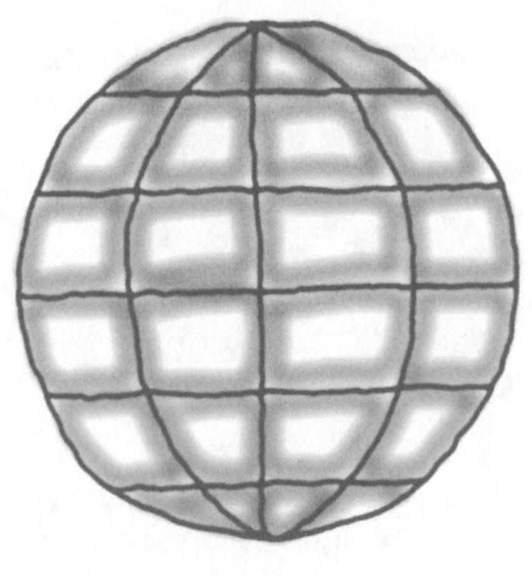

30

Neat!

Acapulco, Mexico, is known for its beautiful beaches, half-moon bay, warm sun, and remarkably blue sky.

On what body of water is Acapulco situated?

Pacific Ocean

Cultural Spanish challenge

Really?

Many towns and cities in the United States have the same name as cities in Spain. The largest of these is in Ohio.

Can you name the city in Ohio that has the same name as a city in Spain?

Toledo

Listen!

El Día de la Raza is celebrated in the Spanish-speaking world in October.

What is this day called in English? What event is being celebrated?

Columbus Day; Columbus's arrival in the New World

Cool!

This stringed instrument is an integral part of all Hispanic music. Spain's Andrés Segovia made it world-popular as a classical instrument as well.

What is this musical instrument?

guitar

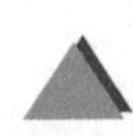

Neat!

This large, beautiful piece of lace adorns the head of Spanish women dressed in the traditional *flamenco* or *sevillana* style.

It may be held in place by an elegant comb and is often worn in church throughout the Hispanic world.

What is the name of this lace head covering?

mantilla

Fact!

About the size of the state of Washington, this is the smallest Spanish-speaking country in South America. There is only one large city: Montevideo. Almost the entire population is of European descent, largely Spanish and Italian.

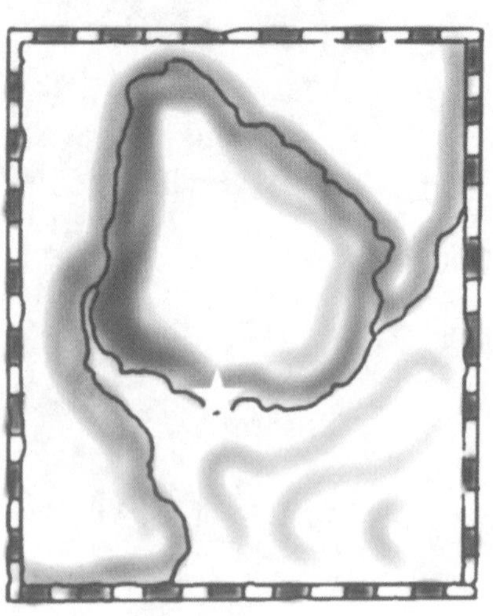

What is this South American country?

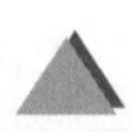

Look!

This famous Calendar Stone was dedicated to the sun god, Tonatiuh. Today, visitors to Mexico City's Museum of Anthropology can marvel at the beauty of this huge sculpture.

What group of people crafted this stone?

Aztecs

Neat!

Located in the Andes Mountains of Peru at an altitude of more than 2,700 meters, these ancient ruins are one of the best-preserved archeological sites in South America. They were rediscovered in 1911 by Hiram Bingham.

What is the name of this ancient site? What pre-Columbian people built this city?

Machu Picchu; Incas

Cool!

The music of this popular rock group is based on the Tex-Mex music known as *norteña* (Spanish songs with a German polka beat). The music is characterized by the accordion and the *bajo sexto,* a 12 string guitar.

What is the name of this rock group? (Hint: Their Spanish name means "wolf" in English!)

Los Lobos

Look!

This artist (1746–1828) painted the family and court of Spain's King Carlos IV. He also painted many works that dramatically illustrate the horrors of war.

Who is this Spanish painter?

Francisco de Goya

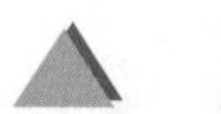

Weird!

This bird, native to the Americas, was called *un guajalote* by the Aztecs. Benjamin Franklin wanted it to be used as the symbol of the United States.

What is this bird?

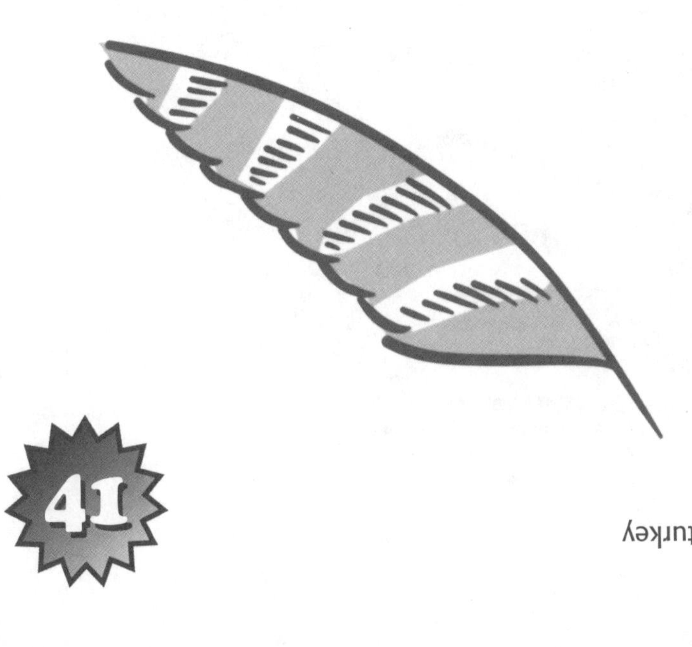

41

turkey

Spanish challenge **Cultural**

Cultural

Spanish challenge

Fact!

This piece of land in southern Spain has been a British possession since 1704. It is only 2.3 square miles in size, and most of it is taken up by a huge limestone mass.

What is the name of this British possession and its most famous geographical feature?

Gibraltar; Rock of Gibraltar

Listen!

This great Puerto Rican baseball player led the Pittsburgh Pirates to the World Series championship in 1960. He died in a plane wreck in 1972 while bringing aid to the victims of a disastrous earthquake in Nicaragua.

Who was this Hall of Famer?

Roberto Clemente

Neat!

One of the most important holidays in Hispanic cultures is *Carnaval.* It is celebrated with parades, music, and dancing in the streets.

What religious holiday is being celebrated at *Carnaval?*

Shrove Tuesday (the day before Ash Wednesday, beginning of the 40 days of Lent, during which traditionally Christians could not eat meat)

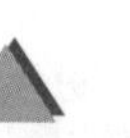

Look!

This Colombian artist (b. 1932) is known for his huge, inflated-looking figures. His paintings of oversized people and his large, whimsical sculptures attract crowds everywhere.

Who is this talented Colombian?

Fernando Botero

Cool!

He is considered to be the father of fusion Latin rock and was one of the first Latino musicians to become popular with mainstream U.S. audiences. One of his best-known songs is "You've Got to Change Your Evil Ways."

Who is this musician?

Carlos Santana

Fact!

Over 90 percent of Chile's population lives in or near this city. It is the capital, as well as the cultural, political, and financial center of the country.

What is the name of this city?

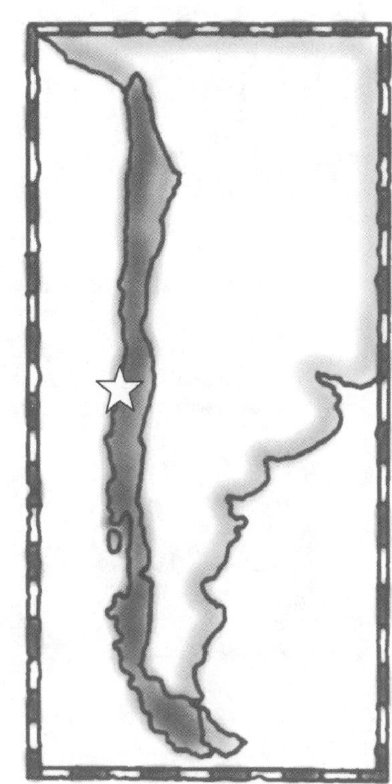

Listen!

An Italian, Luciano Pavarotti, and two Spanish opera stars have given a series of very popular open-air concerts. They are known as "The Three Tenors."

Who are the two Spanish tenors?

Plácido Domingo and José Carreras

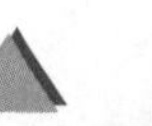
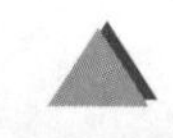

Neat!

This is one of Europe's most popular sports. A Spaniard, Miguel Induráin, won its most famous event—the Tour de France—for the fifth time in 1995.

What sport is this?

bicycle racing

Cultural Spanish challenge

Look!

This Mexican painter (1910–1954) is known for paintings that explore the sadness and pain she experienced in her very difficult life. Her husband was one of Mexico's most famous muralists.

Who is this painter? What was her husband's name?

Frida Kahlo; Diego Rivera

Spanish challenge Cultural

Really?

This Latin American hero (1783–1830) led several South American countries in their fight for independence from Spain. The Republic of Bolivia was named in his honor.

Who was he? What other countries did he help to liberate

Simón Bolívar; Peru, Ecuador, Colombia, and Venezuela

Cool!

This popular Cuban-American singer brought the Latin beat to millions through the band Miami Sound Machine.

Who is this talented singer?

Gloria Estefan

Fact!

The North American Free Trade Agreement (NAFTA) allows for more consumer products to be sold freely among three countries.

What three countries are part of NAFTA?

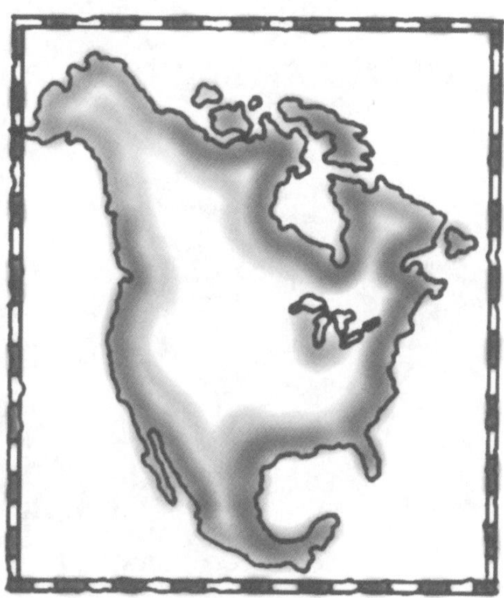

the United States, Canada, and Mexico

Neat!

These small groups walk around as they sing traditional ballads, accompanying themselves on a violin, a small guitar called a *guitarrillo,* a large guitar called a *guitarrón,* and often a trumpet.

What are these musical groups called?

mariachis

Spanish challenge Cultural

Fact!

With a population of 5,000,000, this is the second largest city in Mexico. It is famous as the home of the *mariachis* and for murals by the painter Orozco.

What city is this? Of what Mexican state is it the capital?

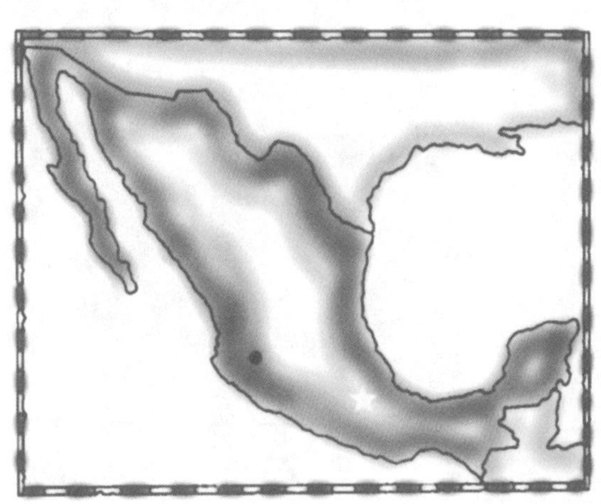

Guadalajara; Jalisco

Listen!

In the Marine Hymn, the line "From the halls of Montezuma" refers to the 1847 U.S. invasion of a Spanish-speaking country.

To what country does this line refer? "Montezuma" is an incorrect form of "Moctezuma." To what or to whom does that refer?

Mexico; Moctezuma (1456–1520) was the Aztec chief defeated by the army of Hernán Cortés in 1519.

    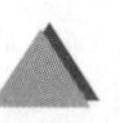 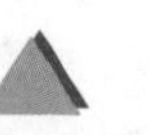 

Look!

This Spaniard (1881–1973) is probably the most famous artist of the twentieth century. His daughter, Paloma, is also an artist, best known for the jewelry she designs.

Who is this Spanish artist?

Pablo Picasso

Fact!

Several U.S. states are very near Spanish-speaking countries.

What Spanish-speaking country is Florida close to? Which states share a border with a Spanish-speaking country? What country is it?

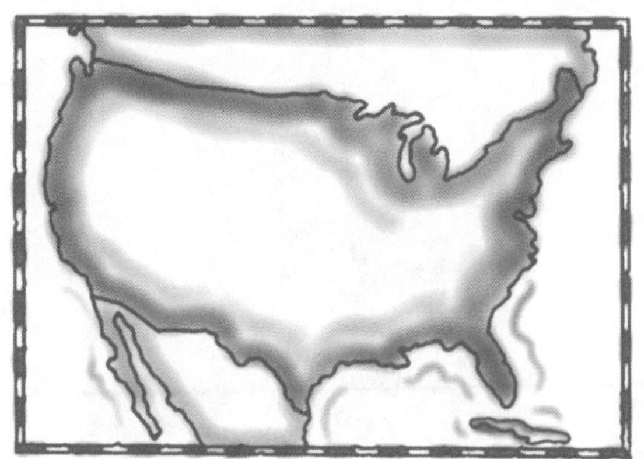

Cuba; California, Arizona, New Mexico, Texas; Mexico

   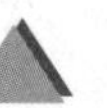 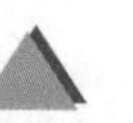  

Really?

This man (1778–1842) does not have what we think of as a Spanish-sounding surname. Yet he is one of the great heroes in South America's movement toward independence from Spain.

Who is this man? What country did he help to liberate?

Bernardo O'Higgins; Chile

Neat!

This beloved Mexican comedian (1911–1995) was born Mario Moreno. His films are known and loved throughout the Spanish-speaking world.

What is the movie name of this comedian?

Cantinflas

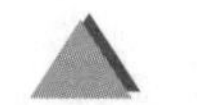

Look!

This neighborhood in Mexico City is known for its art galleries, shops, discotheques, and restaurants. Near it is the famous statue of *El Ángel de la Independencia.*

What is this area called?

La Zona Rosa

Spanish challenge Cultural

Neat!

This colorfully decorated party decoration is made of papier-mâché covered with bright crêpe paper. It is filled with candy and small gifts, and blindfolded partygoers try to break it with a stick.

What is the name of this festive decoration?

piñata

Spanish challenge Cultural

Listen!

The *quinceañera* is an event that a girl's family gives in her honor. It often includes a Mass at church followed by a party with food and dancing.

What event is being celebrated?

¡FELIZ CUMPLEAÑOS!

the girl's fifteenth birthday

Cultural Spanish challenge

Really?

This game, which originated in Spain, is very fast and dangerous. Players wear a basket *(una cesta)* on one hand and try to catch a small, hard ball that can travel up to 150 miles per hour.

What is the name of this exciting sport?

¡jai alai!

Who Knew?

When referring to Mexico City, the Mexicans use the abbreviation D.F.

What do those initials stand for? (Hint: it is similar to D.C. in the United States.)

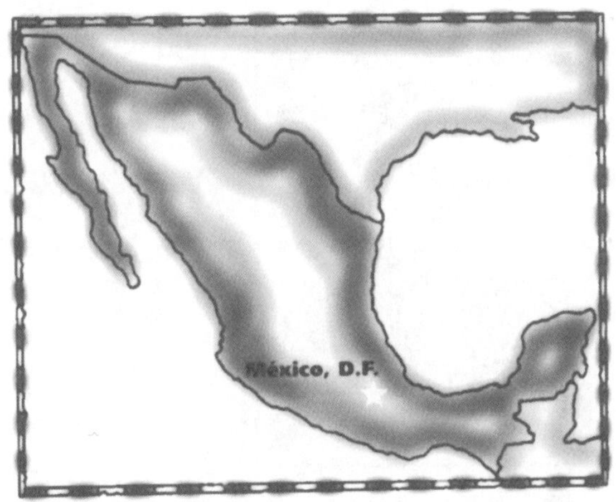

Distrito Federal

Look!

This poet (1853–1895) was imprisoned as a teenager for revolutionary activities. He lived in New York City for several years but returned to his homeland to help lead its fight for independence from Spain. He was killed during that war.

Who was this poet and patriot? Of which country is he the national hero?

José Martí; Cuba

Really?

Names in the Spanish-speaking world contain a lot of information about the family. Suppose your friend was named José Luis Pardo Arnaz.

What is his mother's family name? What is his father's family name? If he introduced himself using only two names, what would they most likely be?

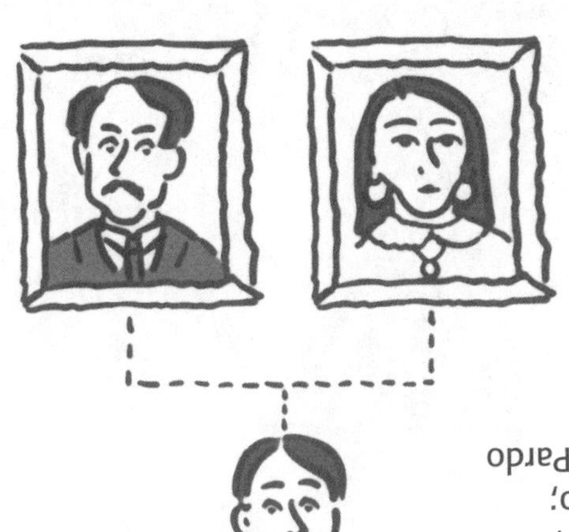

Arnaz;
Pardo;
José Pardo

Cultural Spanish challenge

Cool!

In July, skiers from around the world, including the United States Ski Team, go to Bariloche, Chile, to ski.

Why do they go there in July? If they returned to Bariloche in January, what kind of weather might they expect?

Below the equator, it is winter in July; it would be warm (summer)

      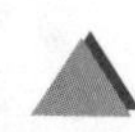

Listen!

Miami, Florida, is well-known for many things, among them its vibrant Cuban community.

What is the name of the famous street that is the heart of Miami's "Little Havana"?

Calle Ocho (8th Street)

Cultural Spanish challenge

Really?

When Spanish speakers refer to *Mexico,* they might be speaking of one of three Mexicos! One of the three is the country itself.

What are the other two?

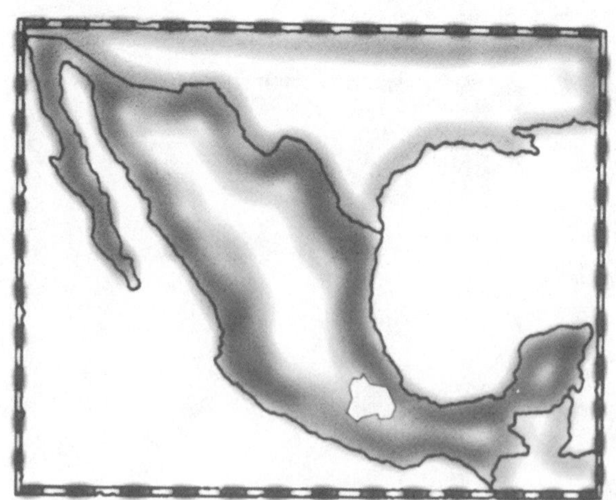

Mexico City (*México, D.F.*, or *la Ciudad de México*) or the State of Mexico (*el estado de México*)

    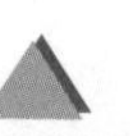  

Spanish challenge Cultural

Look!

El Morro is a massive sixteenth-century Spanish fortress. Its walls are 140 feet high and 20 feet thick! You can see this well-preserved fortress if you visit this Caribbean island.

In which capital city can you find El Morro?

San Juan, Puerto Rico

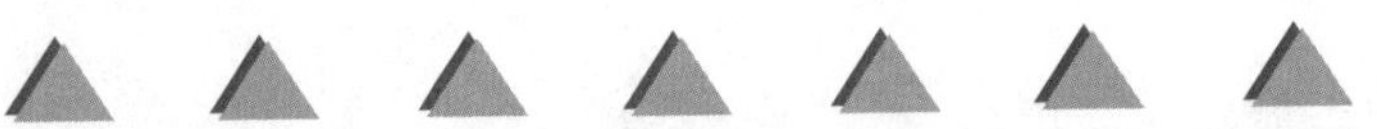

Fact!

The Arabs occupied Spain from 711 until 1492. This occupation of nearly 800 years contributed to the cultural richness of Spain.

The Arabs were driven out during the *Reconquista* by what Spanish king and queen?

Ferdinand and Isabella
(Fernando e Isabel)

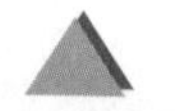      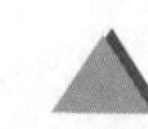

Listen!

The United States has benefited from the immigration of people from throughout the Spanish-speaking world. Three countries are particularly well represented among our population.

What country did most Spanish speakers in Los Angeles come from? How about Miami? And New York?

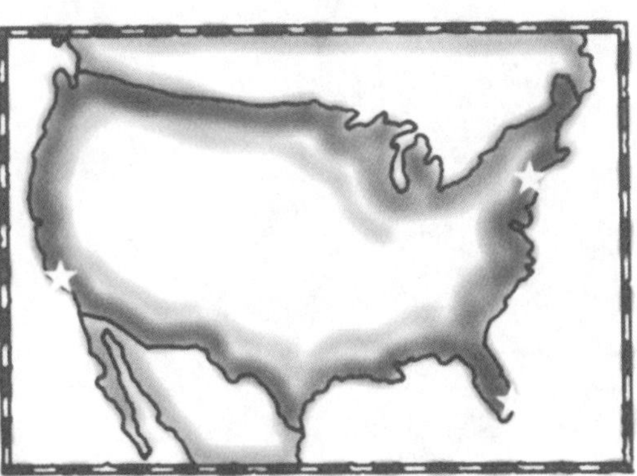

Mexico; Cuba; Puerto Rico

Cultural Spanish challenge

Neat!

This Spanish architect (1852–1926) is famous for his unique style, which blends elements of Gothic art and art nouveau to produce wavy, flowing forms.

Who is this architect? In what Spanish city would you find most of his works?

Antonio Gaudí; Barcelona

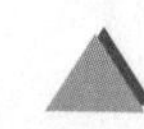

Spanish challenge **Cultural**

Listen!

Travelers in the Spanish-speaking world need to understand the 24-hour clock.

If you saw these departure times on a train schedule, at what time would the trains be leaving?

07:23
14:45
21:12
23:00

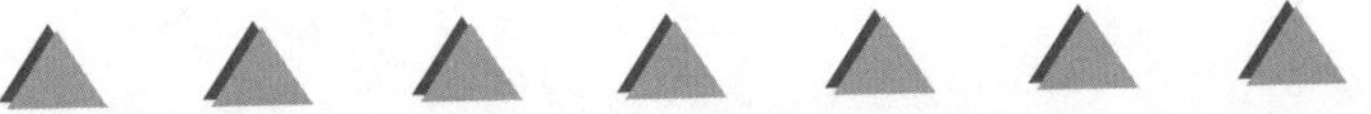

Really?

Schools in Mexico use a different grading system than in the United States.

If you were studying in Mexico and received a grade of 5 and a grade of 9, of which would you be prouder?

the grade of 9 (the grading system is 1–10)

Cool!

Dance is part of nearly every festivity in Spanish-speaking countries. Can you match the dance to the country where it originated?

la bamba	a. Argentina
flamenco	b. Mexico
la salsa	c. Puerto Rico
tango	d. Spain

la bamba–b; flamenco–d; la salsa–c; tango–a

Fact!

Tenochtitlán was a large capital city dating to the early fourteenth century. Today it lies beneath the center of a major Latin American capital.

What city is built on the ruins of Tenochtitlán? Of what indigenous people was Tenochtitlán the capital?

Mexico City; Aztecs

      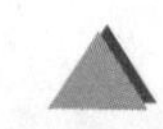

Look!

This Mexican artist (1886–1957) is known for his murals depicting Mexican history and the struggle of the working classes. He often included self-portraits in his murals.

Who was this world-famous artist?

Diego Rivera

Cultural Spanish challenge

Neat!

In many Spanish-speaking countries it is customary to have a fairly sizable late-afternoon snack.

What is this snack called? Why doesn't it spoil people's appetite for dinner?

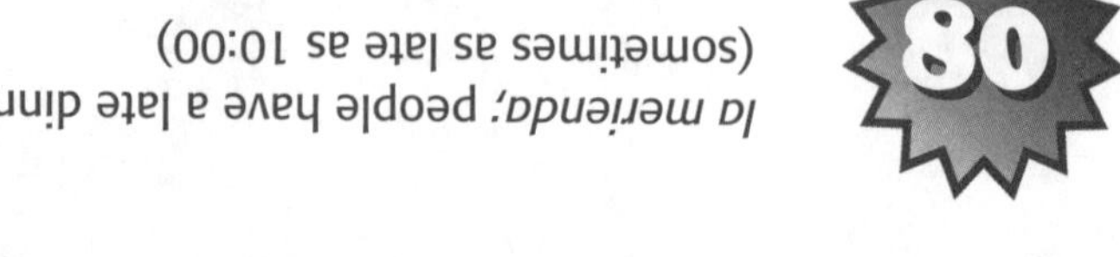

 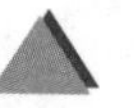  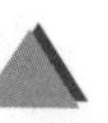  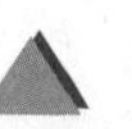 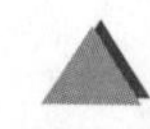

Weird!

The bean from which this food comes was used as money among the Aztecs, who called the drink they made from it *tchocolátl.* We know it as a sweet, but it is naturally bitter.

What do we call this food today?

chocolate

Fact!

The British have ruled these islands east of Argentina since 1833. Argentina, however, still claims them, and the two nations even fought a war over their control in 1982.

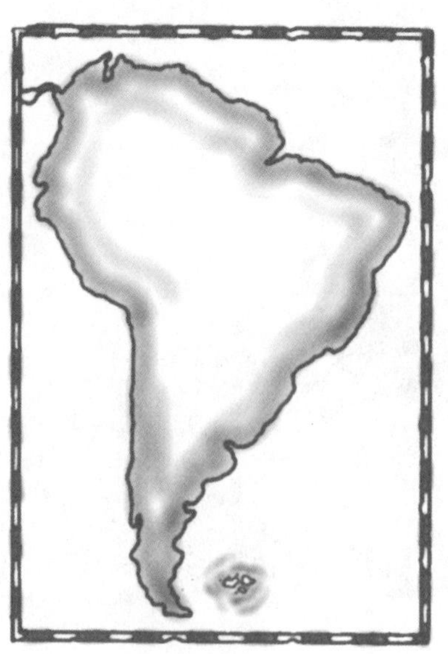

What are the islands called in English? What is their Spanish name?

Falkland Islands; *las Malvinas*

    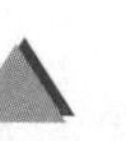 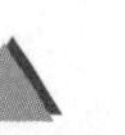 

Listen!

In many Spanish-speaking countries there is a special high-school curriculum for students planning to attend college. In some places it requires an additional year of study.

What is this high-school degree called?

el bachillerato

Spanish challenge **Cultural**

Cool!

Soccer is the most popular sport in the Spanish-speaking world. The most important international tournament is played every four years and features teams from 32 countries.

What is this tournament called in English? What is its Spanish name?

World Cup; *La Copa Mundial*

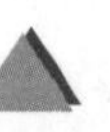
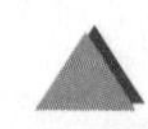

Listen!

Spanish is not the only language of Spain. In the region of Cataluña, for example, Spanish is actually less common than the indigenous language.

In the city of Barcelona, what language would you hear spoken in addition to Spanish?

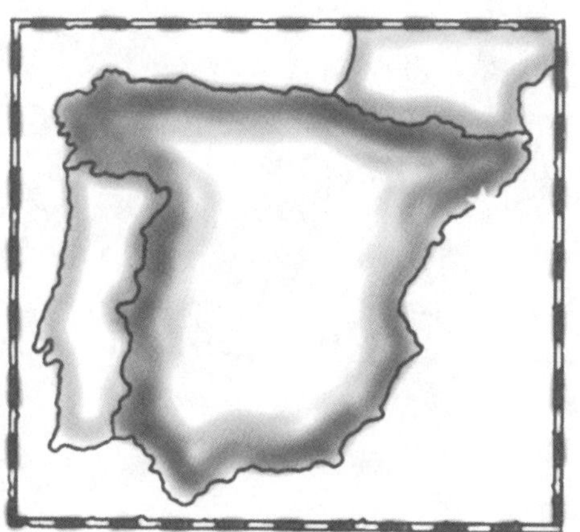

Catalán

Fact!

Spain, like Great Britain, has a form of government called a constitutional monarchy.

Who is the King of Spain? What is the Queen's name?

Juan Carlos; Sofía

Neat!

One of the world's most famous parks is located in Mexico City. It includes an amusement park, several museums, a zoo, and lots of open space.

What is the name of this park?

87

el Bosque de Chapultepec

Spanish challenge **Cultural**

Cultural Spanish challenge

Listen!

Spanish is one of the world's most commonly spoken languages.

Which five countries have the largest Spanish-speaking populations?

1. Mexico, 2. Spain, 3. Colombia, 4. Argentina, 5. United States

  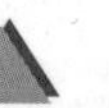  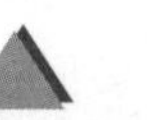 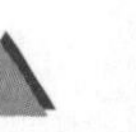

Fact!

This Franciscan priest (1713–1784) founded many missions in California, including San Diego, San Francisco, and Carmel. He is California's representative in Statuary Hall in the U.S. Capitol.

What is the name of this famous missionary?

Fray Junípero Serra

Spanish challenge

Cultural

Cultural Spanish challenge

Look!

This peninsula in eastern Mexico is the site of some of the world's most remarkable ruins.

What is the name of the peninsula? What pre-Columbian people created the civilization whose ruins are today a major tourist attraction?

Yucatán; Mayas

Spanish challenge

Cultural

Who Knew?

In 1994, the Association of Spanish Language Academies voted to eliminate two letters from the Spanish alphabet.

What are these two letters?

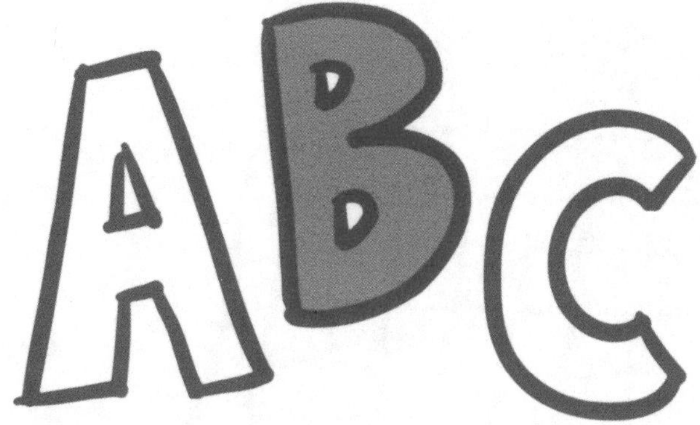

ch (*che*) and ll (*elle*)

Weird!

Calendars in the Spanish-speaking world begin with a different day of the week from those we are accustomed to.

If you looked at a Spanish calendar, what would you see as the first day of the week?

Monday (*lunes*)

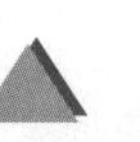

Fact!

Mexico and Central America are extremely mountainous, and many of the mountains are active volcanos.

What is the name of the mountain ranges of Mexico?

Sierra Madre

Cultural Spanish challenge

Look!

This country shares the Iberian Peninsula with Spain and is located on its western border.

What is the capital of this country and what language is spoken there?

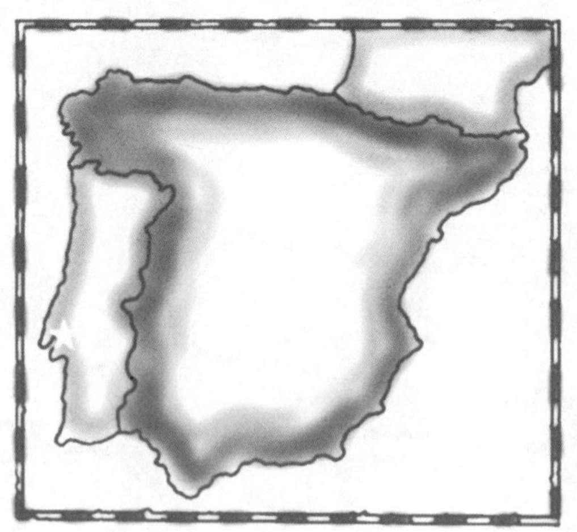

Lisbon; Portuguese

Fact!

The city of Veracruz was settled by the Spanish after Hernán Cortés landed there in 1519. Today, it is an important commercial, industrial, and oil center.

In what country is Veracruz located? On what body of water is it located?

Mexico; Gulf of Mexico (*Golfo de México*)

Really?

This network of roads is 47,516 kilometers long and links 17 Latin American capitals. It was begun in 1925 and completed in 1962.

What is the name of this highway?

Pan American Highway
(*la Panamericana*)

Look!

Doménico Theotokopoulos (1541?–1614) was born in Greece but is one of Spain's most famous artists. His portraits are noted for their elongated bodies, faces, and limbs.

Who was this resident of Toledo? (Hint: His name means "The Greek.")

El Greco

Cultural Spanish challenge

Cultural Spanish challenge

Listen!

Some of our states have Spanish names. These names, for example, mean “colored,” “flowery,” “mountain,” and “snow-covered.”

What four states are these?

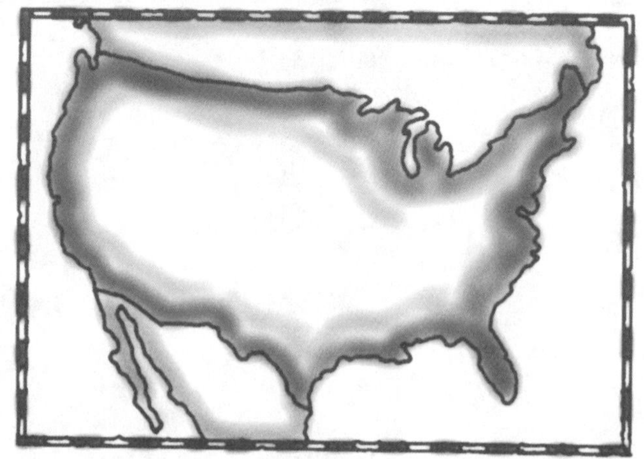

Colorado, Florida, Montana, Nevada

Neat!

In Mexico, it is traditional to be serenaded on this day with the song "Las Mañanitas." It might be sung by friends or by a hired mariachi band.

What event is being celebrated?

99

a birthday (*cumpleaños*)

Cultural Spanish challenge

Fact!

Spain shares a border with France. The two countries are separated by a mountain range.

What is the name of this mountain range?

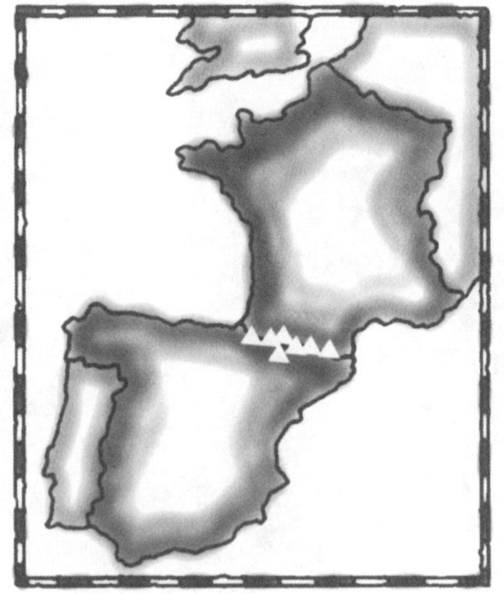

the Pyrenees (*los Pirineos*)

     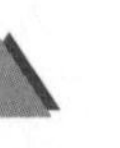 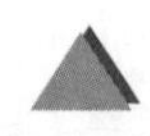

Spanish challenge **Cultural**

Look!

Tierra del Fuego is at the southern tip of South America. It is separated from the mainland by the Strait of Magellan *(el Estrecho de Magallanes)*, which is 563 kilometers long.

What two bodies of water does the Strait of Magellan connect? Tierra del Fuego is part of what two countries?

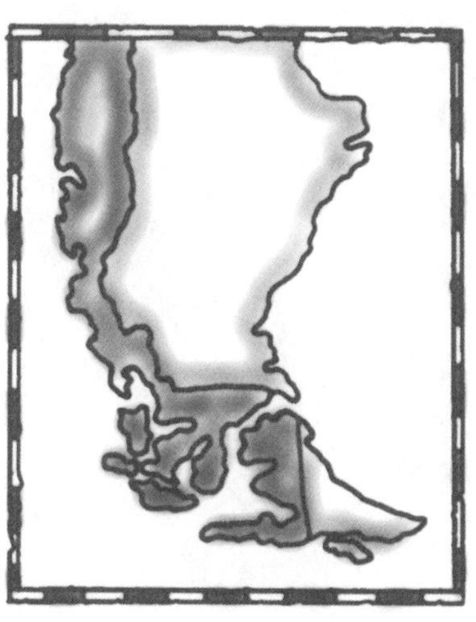

Atlantic and Pacific Oceans; Chile and Argentina

Cultural Spanish challenge

Fact!

Two countries in South America are landlocked.

Which two countries do not have a border on either the Atlantic or Pacific Ocean or on the Caribbean Sea?

Bolivia and Paraguay

Really?

They call it *fútbol* in Spanish.

What do we call this sport in the United States?

soccer

Fact!

This island lies 1,600 kilometers southeast of Florida. In 1493, Columbus named it San Juan Bautista. The original name of its largest city was Spanish for "rich port." Eventually, the two names switched.

What is the name of this Caribbean island today? What is the name of its capital?

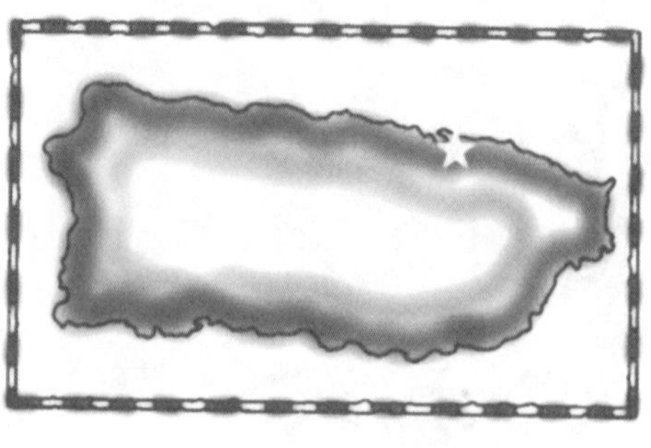

Puerto Rico; San Juan

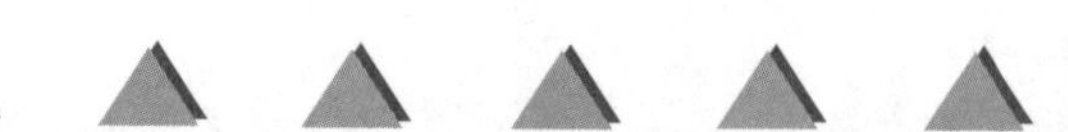

Listen!

In 1519, this Spanish explorer arrived at Tenochtitlán, capital of the Aztec empire. Within two years, he had defeated the Aztecs and established Spanish rule in Mexico.

Who was this *conquistador?*

Hernán Cortés

Cultural Spanish challenge

Neat!

This sport is very popular in Latin America. The players' positions have names such as *lanzador, receptor, cortocampo,* and *bateador designado.*

What sport is this? What is it called in Spanish?

baseball; el béisbol

Spanish challenge Cultural

Who Knew?

This Bolivian teacher gained fame in the U.S. for his success in teaching advanced mathematics to students in the East Los Angeles *barrio. Stand and Deliver,* a film starring Edward James Olmos, tells his story.

Who is this dedicated teacher?

Jaime Escalante

Spanish challenge

Cultural

Listen!

Spanish is called a Romance language. So are French, Italian, Portuguese, and Romanian.

Romance languages came from what other language? Why are they called that?

ESPAÑOL

ITALIANO

FRANCÉS

Latin; Latin was the language of the Roman Empire

  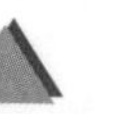   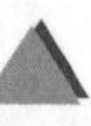 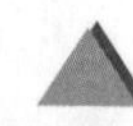

Cool!

This Guatemalan woman won the 1992 Nobel Peace Prize for her condemnation of human rights violations against the indigenous peoples of Central America.

Who is this woman? Of what indigenous group is she a member?

109

Rigoberta Menchú; Quiché

Cultural Spanish challenge

Look!

About 70 kilometers southeast of Mexico City you will find Popocatépetl and Iztaccíhuatl. The former smokes sometimes; the latter doesn't.

Who or what are "Popo" and "Izti"?

volcanos (Popocatépetl is still active)

Cultural Spanish challenge

Fact!

Can you give the dates of these holidays? Are they all widely celebrated in the U.S.? Which ones are celebrated on a different day in the U.S.?

a) el Año Nuevo
b) el Día de los Muertos
c) el Día de la Raza
d) el Día del Trabajo
e) Navidad
f) Nochebuena

a) Jan. 1, b) Nov. 2 (All Souls' Day), c) Oct. 12, d) May 1 (Labor Day), Dec. 25, Dec. 24; All Souls' Day is not widely celebrated in the U.S.; Labor Day in the U.S. is the first Monday in September.

Fact!

This country has two capitals. The government's administrative branch is in the country's largest city. Its judicial branch is in a much smaller city to the southeast.

Which country has two capitals? What are they?

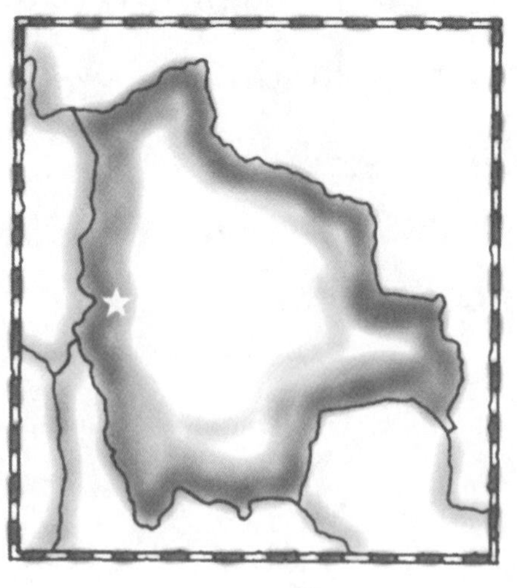

Listen!

In this South American country, much of the indigenous population speaks the Quechua language.

What country is this?

Peru

Neat!

This Mexican silver-mining town is a major tourist attraction. Its steep hills, cobblestone streets, and colonial architecture are a national monument, and it is illegal to build a modern building there.

What is the name of this silver city?

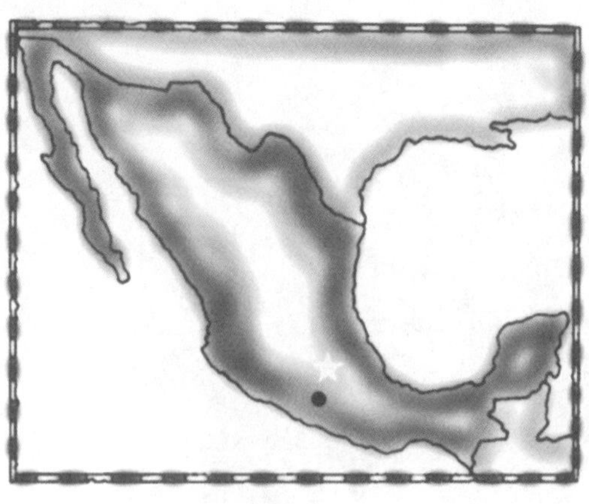

Taxco

Really?

Mexico is the world's sixth largest producer of petroleum. One Spanish-speaking country in South America, however, has even larger oil reserves, and oil represents 80 percent of its exports.

What is this oil-rich nation?

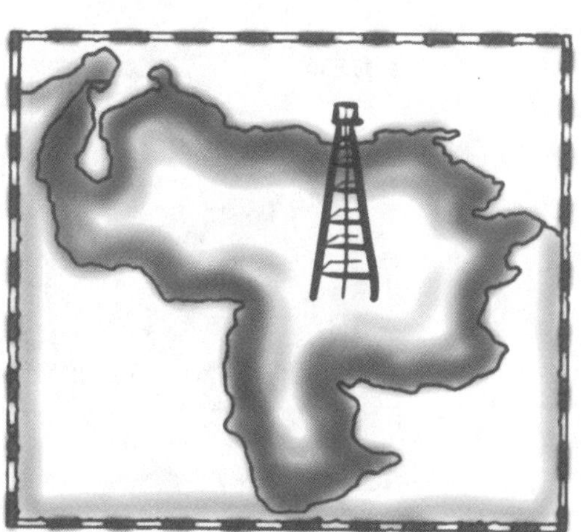

Venezuela

Spanish challenge Cultural

Cultural Spanish challenge

Listen!

This Colombian writer (b. 1928) won the Nobel Prize for Literature in 1982. Several of his works have been very popular in the U.S. For example: *Cien años de soledad* and *El amor en los tiempos de cólera.*

Who is this renowned novelist?

Look!

This Spanish painter (1904–1989) blended reality and fantasy in bizarre, compelling works of art. *La persistencia de la memoria* is one of his most famous works.

Who was this painter?

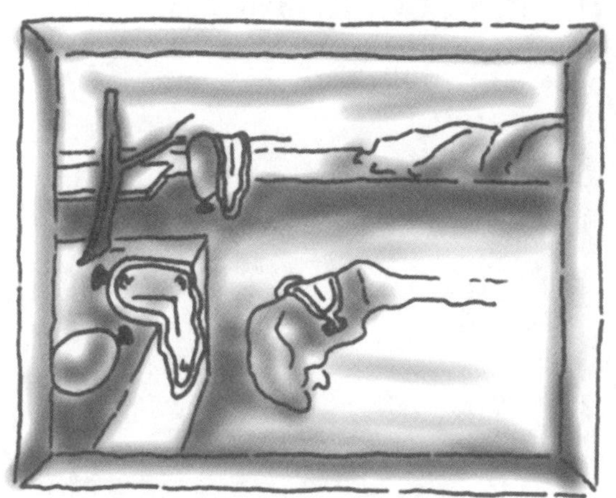

Salvador Dalí

Cultural Spanish challenge

Fact!

The Balearic Islands *(las islas Baleares)* are a major Spanish resort area east of the mainland. The three best known of the islands are Mallorca, Menorca, and Ibiza.

In what body of water will you find these beautiful islands?

Mediterranean Sea *(el mar Mediterráneo)*

Neat!

These islands off the coast of Africa have belonged to Spain since 1479. The largest of them is Tenerife. A type of popular household pet was first found there and named after the islands.

What is the name of these Spanish islands?

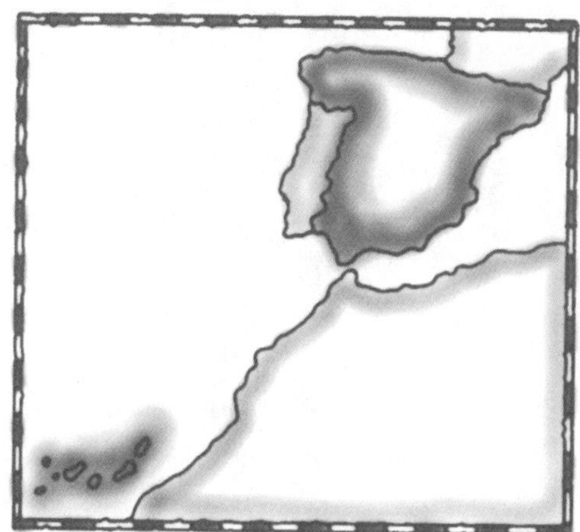

Canary Islands (*las islas Canarias*)

Cultural Spanish challenge

Listen!

The musical world lost a great talent when this popular young Mexican American singer from Texas was killed by a fan in 1995.

Who was this recording artist?

Selena

Look!

The beauty and historical importance of the ancient Mayan ruins of Copán caused them to be named a UNESCO World Heritage Site in 1980.

In which country are these ruins located?

Honduras

Who Knew?

The ancient Popol Vuh chronicles the history of a pre-Columbian civilization that was at its height from approximately A.D. 300–900.

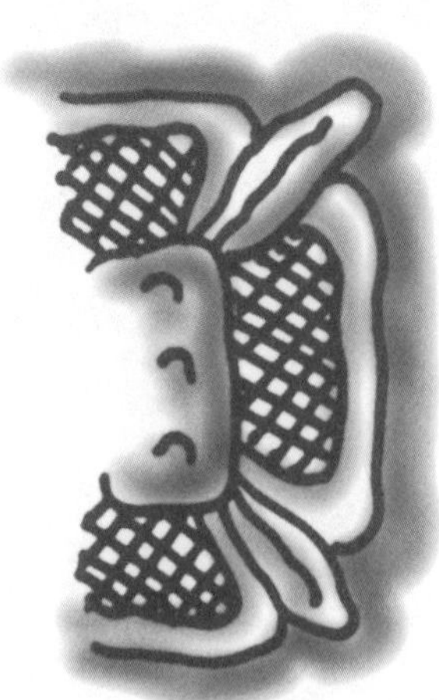

The Popol Vuh tells the story of what people?

the Mayas

Fact!

This once-Spanish city was founded in 1769 as *El Pueblo de Nuestra Señora la Reina de los Ángeles de Porciúncula.* An estimated 18 percent of all Hispanics in the United States live here.

What is the name of this city today?

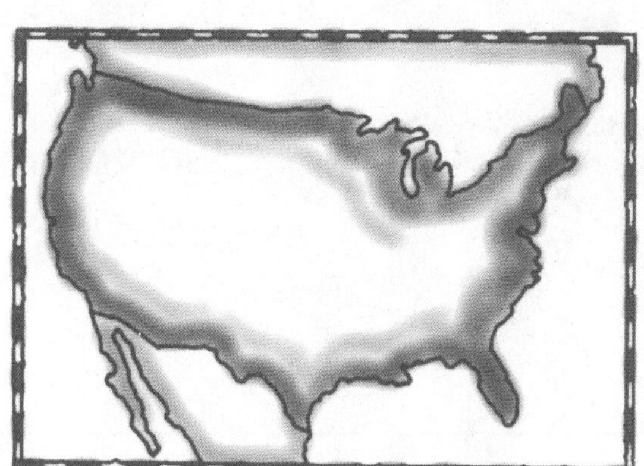

Los Angeles

Cultural Spanish challenge

Cool!

Easter Island *(la isla de Pascua)* lies in the South Pacific, 3,700 kilometers west of South America. It is famous for hundreds of ancient stone statues, some as high as 12 meters and weighing up to 82 metric tons.

Since 1888 this island has been a territory of what South American country?

Chile

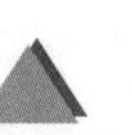

Listen!

You are in the Mayan ruins of Chichén Itzá looking at the remains of buildings and structures whose Spanish names mean the Castle *(El Castillo)*, Temple of the Warriors *(El Templo de los Guerreros)*, and the Snail *(El Caracol)*.

In which country is Chichén Itzá located?

Mexico

Really?

Considered the national drink in some South American countries, *mate* is brewed from the dried leaves of a type of holly. It is drunk through a metallic straw from a beautifully carved and decorated gourd.

Can you name one or more countries where *mate* is drunk?

Look!

You are watching a group of people playing *maracas, marimbas,* and *tambores.*

Are you watching a sport, a card game, or a musical group?

a musical group

Spanish challenge **Cultural**

Fact!

This bloody war (1936–1939) ended in defeat for the Republic. The winning general (1892–1975) then ruled the country until his death. A group of Americans, calling themselves the Lincoln Brigade, fought for the Republic.

What war was this? Who was the winning general who ruled for 36 years?

Spanish Civil War; Francisco Franco

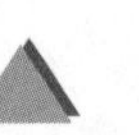

Spanish challenge

Cultural

Look!

The brutal destruction of the small town of Guernica in northern Spain during the Spanish Civil War inspired one of the world's most famous paintings.

Who painted *Guernica?* In what famous Madrid museum would you find it?

Pablo Picasso; the Prado

Fact!

This outstanding Hispanic American (b. 1947) was mayor of San Antonio (1981–1989) and was appointed Secretary of Housing and Urban Development by President Clinton in 1993.

Who is this Hispanic American politician?

Henry Cisneros

Neat!

This Mexican American has a doctorate in electrical engineering specializing in computer science. In 1993, in the space shuttle *Discovery,* she became the first female Hispanic astronaut to orbit Earth.

Who is this astronaut?

Ellen Ochoa

Really?

This river is 6,437 kilometers long and at some points as much as ten kilometers wide. It begins high in the Andes of Peru. Before it empties into the Atlantic Ocean in Northern Brazil, more than 200 rivers flow into it.

What river is this? Which rivers—if any—are longer than it is?

Amazon River; the Nile (6,671 km)

Look!

This talented Puerto Rican actor (1940–1995) may be best known for his role in the popular movies about the Addams Family. He won an Emmy for his portrayal of rain forest activist Chico Mendes.

Who was this fine actor?

Raúl Juliá

Cultural Spanish challenge

Fact!

The largest of the Caribbean Islands lies only 140 kilometers south of Florida. It was visited by Columbus during his first voyage in 1492. Since 1959 it has been ruled by Fidel Castro.

What is the name of this island? What is its capital?

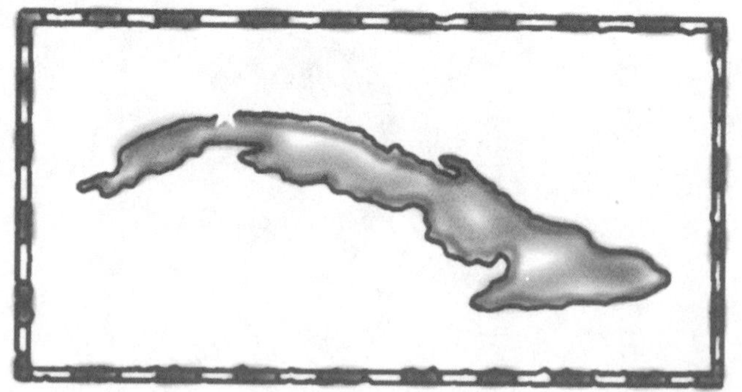

Cuba; Havana (*La Habana*)

Cultural Spanish challenge

Listen!

This is the smallest republic in Central America and the most densely populated. It is the only country in the region that does not border on the Caribbean Sea.

Which country is this?

El Salvador

Neat!

This Mexican president (1806–1872) was a Zapotec Indian. He achieved land reform and the separation of church and state and is called "the Abraham Lincoln of Mexico."

Who was this great leader?

Benito Juárez

Fact!

These cities are the capitals of what South American countries?

a) Asunción	e) Lima
b) Bogotá	f) Montevideo
c) Buenos Aires	g) Quito
d) Caracas	h) Santiago

a) Paraguay,
b) Colombia,
c) Argentina,
d) Venezuela,
e) Peru,
f) Uruguay,
g) Ecuador,
h) Chile

Cultural Spanish challenge

Who Knew?

This country has the highest standard of living in Central America and is known as the region's most stable democracy. It is famous for its ecological policies and large number of national parks.

Which country is this?

Costa Rica

Look!

The most famous and beautiful of Spain's many parks is in its capital city. The park dates to 1630. Today it serves millions of *madrileños* who go there to stroll, picnic, and row on the beautiful lake.

What is the name of this park? In what city is it? What is a *madrileño?*

Buen Retiro (or *El Retiro*); Madrid; a person from Madrid

Cultural Spanish challenge

Really?

Most of the countries of South America use Spanish as their official language. The largest one does not.

What is the largest country in South America? What is its official language?

Brazil; Portuguese

Cultural Spanish challenge

Fact!

These cities are the capitals of what Central American countries?

a) Managua

b) San José

c) Tegucigalpa

a) Nicaragua, b) Costa Rica, c) Honduras

Fact!

This island was ceded by Spain to the United States in 1898 following the Spanish-American War. It is currently a U.S. commonwealth.

What is the name of this island?

Puerto Rico

Listen!

Money, money, money! Can you name the Spanish-speaking countries that have these monetary units as their currency?

What is the most common monetary unit in the Spanish-speaking world?

a) el dólar
b) la peseta
c) el sol
d) el sucre

a) Puerto Rico, b) Spain, c) Peru, d) Ecuador; *el peso* (8 countries)

Cultural Spanish challenge

Who Knew?

El Ebro, el Duero, el Tajo, el Guadiana, el Guadalquivir.

Are these the five most famous resorts in Spain, the five major rivers in Spain, or the five highest mountains in Spain?

rivers

Look!

Mexico is a large country, about the size of the states of Texas, New Mexico, Arizona, Nevada, and California combined.

What country borders Mexico on the north? What two countries border Mexico on the south?

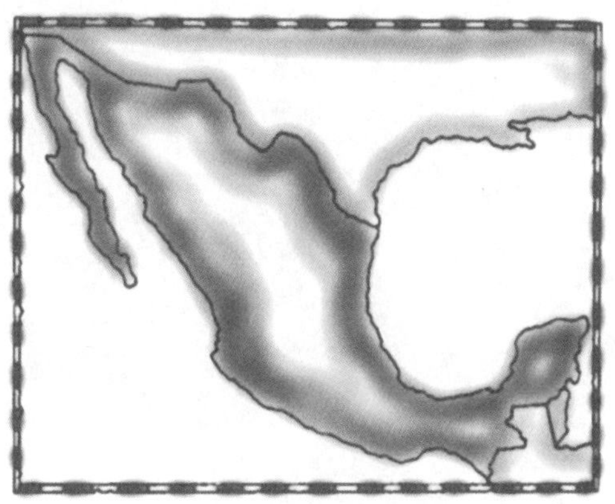

United States; Guatemala and Belize

Spanish challenge

Cultural

Cool!

The Mayan culture was at its peak from A.D. 300–900. This brilliant civilization was the first to use the concept of zero and had a writing system with more than 800 symbols.

Name three countries in which the Mayan civilization thrived.

Mexico, Guatemala, Belize, and Honduras

  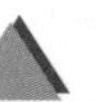    

Look!

El Yunque is the only rain forest that is part of the U.S. National Park Service.

Where would you go to visit El Yunque?

Puerto Rico

Spanish challenge **Cultural**

Cultural Spanish challenge

Really?

At an altitude of 3,660 meters above sea level, this is the highest capital city in the world.

What city is this? Of what country is it the capital?

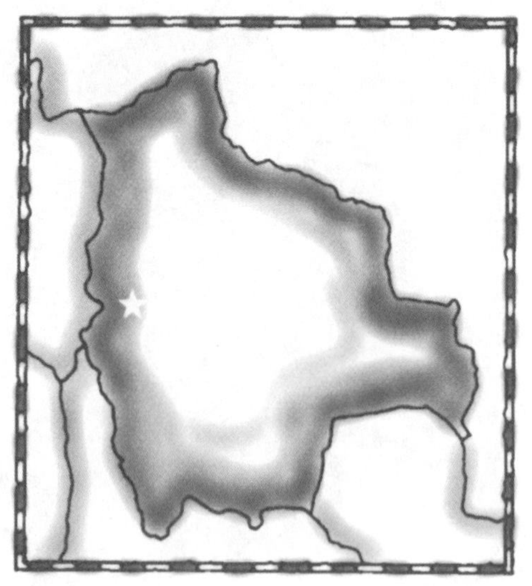

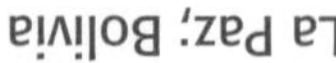

Listen!

This South American Indian people ruled one of the largest and richest empires in the Americas. Their capital was Cuzco, in southern Peru. They were conquered by the Spaniards in 1532.

Who were these people? What Spanish *conquistador* defeated them?

Incas; Francisco Pizarro

Cultural Spanish challenge

Look!

The flag of Spain contains two bright colors in three horizontal bands, with a coat of arms on the central band.

What are the colors of the Spanish flag?

two red bands and one yellow band

Weird!

This animal of the South American jungle is known for moving very slowly among the trees. Its Spanish name is *perezoso.* In both English and Spanish its name translates to lazy!

What is this animal?

151

sloth

Cultural Spanish challenge

Neat!

This beautiful bird is found in the jungles of Central America. Its tail feathers were highly valued by the Aztecs, whose emperors used them in their crowns.

What is the name of this bird? Which country has named its currency after the bird?

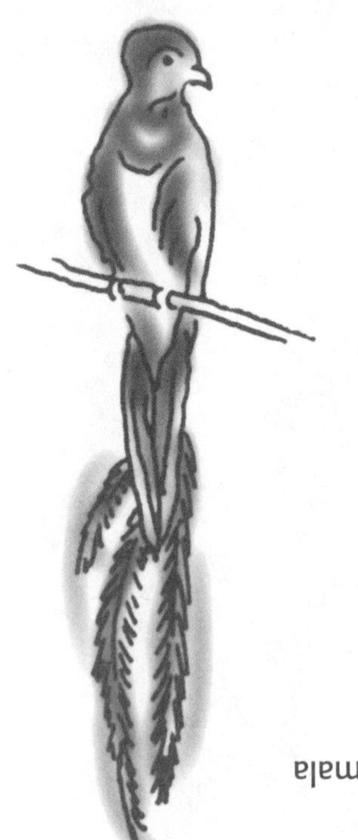

quetzal; Guatemala

Really?

At 979 meters, Angel Falls *(el Salto Angel)* is the highest waterfall in the world. It was named for an American pilot, Jimmy Angel, who first saw it in 1935.

In what country is Angel Falls located?

Venezuela

Cool!

This Spanish-born film director (1900–1983) lived in Mexico for many years. Oddly, he is perhaps best known for three films he made in France: *Un chien andalou* (1929), which he made with Salvador Dalí; *Belle de jour* (1966); and the Oscar winner, *Le Charme discret de la bourgeoisie* (1972).

Who was this highly respected director?

Listen!

This Spaniard (1500–1542) explored Central America, was a leader with Pizarro when he conquered the Incas, and was appointed governor of Cuba by the King of Spain. He later explored the southern U.S.

Who was this Spanish explorer? In May, 1541, he became the first European to see what major river?

Cultural Spanish challenge

Listen!

You will find the influence of the Spanish explorers and their religion in the names of cities in the United States. For example, *San* and *Santa* are the Spanish words for "saint."

How many U.S. cities can you list that have Spanish names for saints? In each case, was the saint male or female?

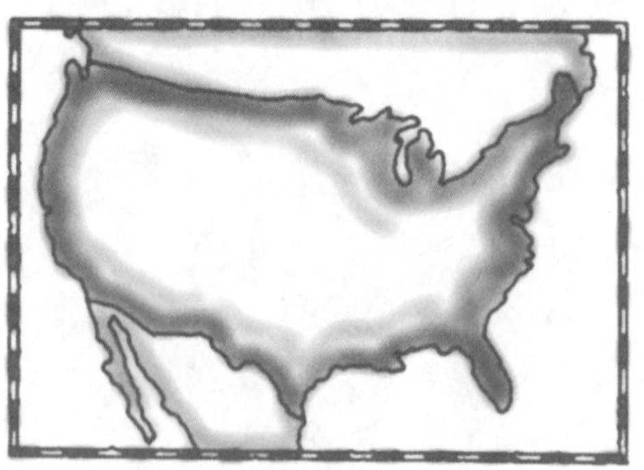

Answers will vary; *San* precedes a masculine name, *Santa* a feminine name.

    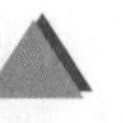  

Really?

The *gauchos* are cowboys of the South American plains, and they are just as legendary as U.S. cowboys! In one country, the plains are called *las pampas*.

What is this country?

157

Argentina

Fact!

South America is bordered by three large bodies of water. Only one country has a coastline on two of them.

What is this country? What are the two bodies of water?

Colombia; Pacific Ocean and Caribbean Sea

     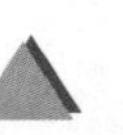 

Spanish challenge Cultural

Who Knew?

If you are in Spain on New Year's Eve, it is customary to eat 12 of these as the clock strikes midnight.

What fruit are you eating?

grapes

Fact!

This shallow lake is the largest in South America and is famous for the oil derricks rising from its surface.

What is this lake? In what country is it located?

Lake Maracaibo (*el Lago Maracaibo*);
Venezuela

Look!

In 1540, this Spanish explorer (1510–1554) traveled northward from Mexico in search of the legendary golden Seven Cities of Cibola. He failed in that, but he and his men became the first Europeans to see Arizona, New Mexico, Texas, Oklahoma, and Kansas.

Who was this famous explorer?

Fernando Vásquez de Coronado

Cool!

This Cuban-born singer received a Master of Arts degree in jazz vocal performance and sang backup vocals for the Miami Sound Machine. His first two hits, "Just Another Day" and "Angel," reached the Top 40.

Who is this talented singer?

Jon Secada

Fact!

Peru and Bolivia are each bordered by five countries.

Which five countries border on Peru? Which five share a border with Bolivia?

Ecuador, Colombia, Brazil, Bolivia, and Chile; Peru, Brazil, Paraguay, Argentina, and Chile

Neat!

This Cuban-born band leader was co-star with his wife of one of the most popular comedy shows in television history. Nearly fifty years later, it is still seen regularly throughout the world.

Who was this television star? What was his wife's name? What was their first hit show called?

Really?

The Mexican flag depicts the mythical founding of the ancient city of Tenochtitlán through the symbol of an eagle with a snake in its mouth sitting on a cactus. There are three vertical bands on the flag.

What are the colors of the bands on the Mexican flag?

green, white, and red (*verde, blanco y rojo*)

Look!

On September 29, 1513, this Spanish explorer (1475–1517), guided by local Indians, waded into the Pacific Ocean and claimed all the land touching its eastern coast for Spain.

Who was this first European to see the Pacific Ocean?

Vasco Núñez de Balboa

  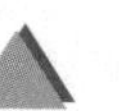   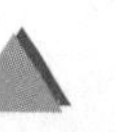 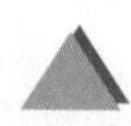

Spanish challenge

Cultural

Fact!

This Central American republic is about the size of Louisiana and has coasts on both the Pacific Ocean and the Caribbean. It has historically had the poorest economy in Central America.

What is the name of this country?

Honduras

Cultural Spanish challenge

Neat!

Many Spanish-speaking people celebrate their *santo* with greater festivity than their *cumpleaños.*

What is a person's *santo?* What is one's *cumpleaños?*

saint's day (the day in the Church calendar honoring the saint who has the same name as that person); birthday

 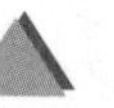 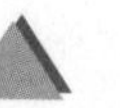 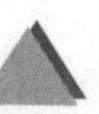 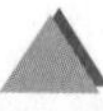 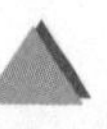 

Spanish challenge

Cultural

Listen!

Guaraní is, with Spanish, one of this country's two official languages. The country's monetary unit is also called the *guaraní.*

What country is this? Where does the word *guaraní* come from?

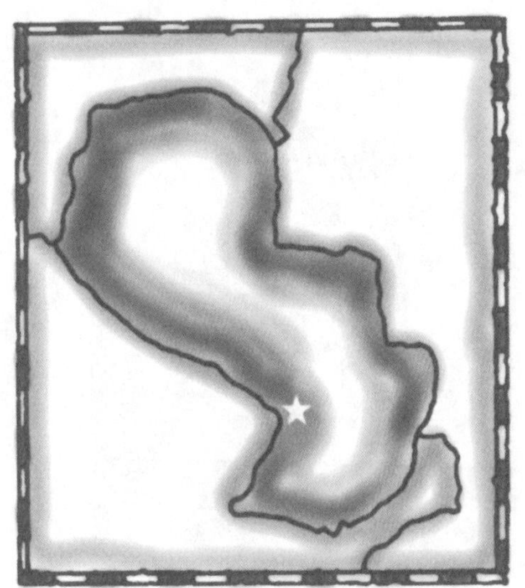

Paraguay; the Guaraní Indians

Cultural Spanish challenge

Look!

There are two very large lakes in this Central American country. One has the same name as the country. The other has the same name as the capital city.

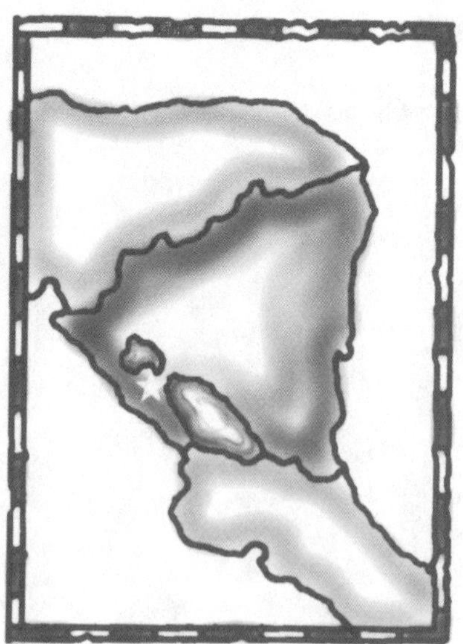

What two lakes are these?

Fact!

The Pyrenees separate Spain from France. Lying in this mountain range is one of the smallest countries in the world. It is governed jointly by France and Spain.

What is the name of this country?

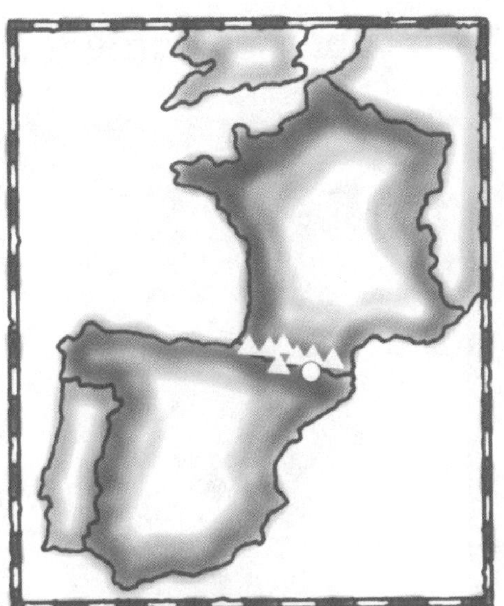

Andorra

Really?

This is the deepest and second largest lake in South America. At an altitude of 3,815 meters, it is the highest navigable lake in the world.

What is the name of the lake? What two countries border on it?

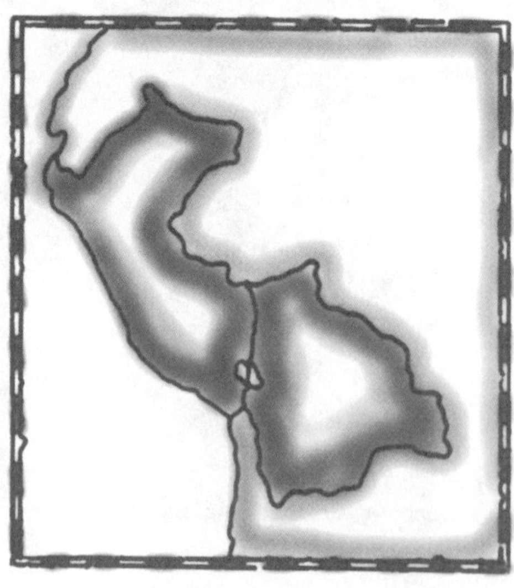

Weird!

This novel was published in two parts in 1605 and 1615. In it, the hero imagines himself a knight in armor. He attacks windmills that he thinks are giants and flocks of sheep he mistakes for an army.

Who wrote this literary masterpiece? What is its name? In the book, who is the knight's faithful companion?

Miguel de Cervantes; *Don Quixote;* Sancho Panza

Really?

This engineering marvel allows ships to pass between the Atlantic and Pacific Oceans without traveling all the way around South America. It was built by the United States between 1904 and 1914.

What is this remarkable engineering achievement?

Panama Canal

Spanish challenge **Cultural**

Cool!

This city in northern Spain is famous for *la Fiesta de San Fermín* and the running of the bulls.

What city is this? On what date is this fiesta celebrated?

Pamplona; July 7

Fact!

Can you match these countries and their monetary units? After what or whom were each of these currencies named?

Costa Rica	a. el balboa
El Salvador	b. el bolívar
Nicaragua	c. el colón
Panama	d. el córdoba
Venezuela	

Costa Rica–c; El Salvador–c; Nicaragua–d; Panama–a; Venezuela–b; Balboa (see Q. 164), Bolívar (see Q. 49), Colón (see Q. 2), Francisco Fernández de Córdoba (1475?–1526?) who established the Nicaraguan cities of León and Granada

Who Knew?

This museum in Madrid houses one of the finest art collections in the entire world.

What is the name of this museum?

the Prado

Spanish challenge Cultural

Neat!

Spain has a very extensive coastline, particularly on the Mediterranean Sea. The beautiful beaches attract tourists year-round. *La Costa del Sol* is one of the most famous coastal regions of Spain.

Can you name another famous Mediterranean coastal region of Spain?

la Costa Blanca, la Costa Brava, la Costa de la Luz, la Costa del Azahar, and la Costa Dorada

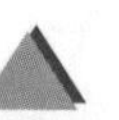

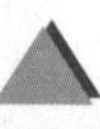

Look!

There are more than 200 waterfalls on South America's Río Paraná. The most magnificent—72 meters high and three kilometers wide—are on the border between Argentina and Brazil.

What is the name of these falls?

Iguaçú Falls (el Salto Grande de *Santa María*)

Spanish challenge **Cultural**

Cultural Spanish challenge

Who Knew?

Iberia is one of the largest peninsulas in the world.

On what continent is the Iberian Peninsula? What would you find there?

Europe; Spain and Portugal

Fact!

This narrow country is almost twice the size of Montana, but only 427 kilometers wide at its widest point. The northern three-sevenths of the country is desert. The southern three-sevenths is a rocky region of dense forests, lakes, and glaciers.

What country is this? What is the name of its southernmost point?

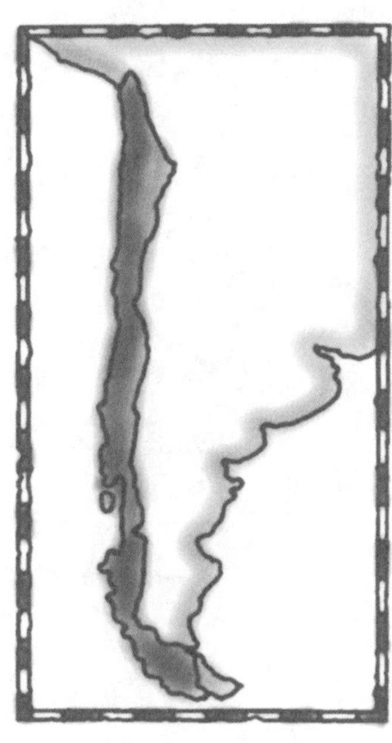

Chile; Cape Horn (*el Capo de Hornos*)

Neat!

They live in the Pyrenees region of northern Spain and southern France. They speak their own unique language (Euskera) and have given the world the beret and the game of jai alai.

Bilbao and San Sebastián are the two largest cities of the region.

Who are these people? What is the region called where they live?

Basques (*los vascos*); the Basque country (*el país vasco*)

Fact!

There's only one national flag in the world whose two sides are not identical. The difference is that while the seal in the front is the Nation's Seal, the one on the reverse is the Seal of the Treasury. Can you name that South American country?

Paraguay

Cultural Spanish challenge

Who Knew?

In Peru, people can travel by train to the ruins of Machu Picchu. The railway also leads to the highest train station in the world, at 4,818 meters above sea level in the Andes. Do you know the name of this station?

Ticlio

Cool!

In 1980, Adolfo Pérez Esquivel (b. 1931) received the Nobel Peace Prize for his efforts in the defense of human rights. A scholar and peace activist, he also received the Pope John XXIII Peace Memorial Award among other distinctions. In what country was Esquivel born?

Argentina

Neat!

In the United States, the President's house is the White House (*La Casa Blanca*). Argentina's government house is known as La Casa Rosada (*The Pink House*). In Venezuela, the country's Foreign Ministry is housed on what originally was a Royal Prison. This building also receives its name from a color. Can you name the building?

La Casa Amarilla (The Yellow House)

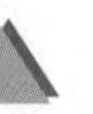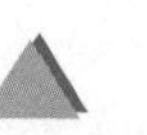

Fact!

The organization of the first Soccer World Cup in 1930 was granted to a South American country to honor its achievements in international sports and the centennial celebration of the country's constitution. Can you name this country?

Uruguay

Really?

The capital city of Ecuador is located at 2,830 meters above sea level and surrounded by many snow-peaked mountains. However, because it enjoys mild temperatures and cool breezes year round it has been named the City of Eternal Spring. What is Ecuador's capital city?

Quito

Cool!

Carved out of mountainous jungle, the *Ciudad Perdida* (Lost City) was built around 500 years BC by the Tayrona Indians. Hidden by the thick canopy, only the descendants of its builders knew about it until it was "discovered" in the 1970's. It's been declared a national treasure. In what country is it located?

Colombia

Cultural Spanish challenge

Really?

In Spanish-speaking countries, the phrase "*Vale un Perú*" (It's worth as much as Perú) is used to describe something or someone of immeasurable worth. Can you guess what the origin of this expression might be?

It dates back to the times when seemingly endless riches were found in Perú by the conquistadors.

 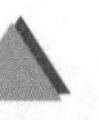     

Listen!

When the Spanish first arrived at a group of islands in the Caribbean they thought the islands were surrounded by shallow water, so they used the words *Baja Mar* to name them. The islands' current name derives from those two words. Do you know what these islands are?

191

The Bahamas

Weird!

One legend concerning the mariachi traces this musical tradition back to the occupation of Mexico by a foreign power. It contends that the Spanish name *mariachi* was derived from "*mariages*" (wedding), since having a musical group at weddings was customary at that time. According to this legend, what language is mariachi derived from?

French